ROCKS: The Hard Facts

Unearthing Metamorphic Rocks

Willa Dee

PowerKiDS press

New York

Published in 2014 by The Rosen Publishing Group, Inc.
29 East 21st Street, New York, NY 10010

First Edition

Editor: Jennifer Way
Book Design: Kate Vlachos
Photo Research: Katie Stryker

Photo Credits: Cover Daniele Carotenuto Photography/Flickr/Getty Images; pp. 4, 6 iStockphoto/Thinkstock; pp. 5, 21 (left) Doug Lemke/Shutterstock.com; p. 7 Karen Grigoryan/Shutterstock.com; p. 8 Vulkanette/Shutterstock.com; p. 9 (top) Woudloper/Wikimedia Commons/File: http://commons.wikimedia.org/wiki/File:Igneous_structures.jpg; p. 9 (bottom) Ryan McVay/Digital Vision/Thinkstock; p. 10 Joel Arem/Photo Researchers/Getty Images; p. 11 Karen Wunderman/Shutterstock.com; p. 12 assistant/Shutterstock.com; p. 13 Shulevskyy Volodymyr/Shutterstock.com; p. 14 (left) Visuals Unlimited, Inc./Dr. Marli Miller/Visuals Unlimited/Getty Images; p. 14 (right) James Steinberg/Photo Researchers/Getty Images; p. 15 Zern Liew/Shutterstock.com; p. 17 (top) LesPalenik/Shutterstock.com; p. 17 (bottom) villorejo/Shutterstock.com; p. 18 Belozorova Elena/Shutterstock.com; p. 19 Marafona/Shutterstock.com; p. 20 Alexandra Lande/Shutterstock.com; p. 21 (right) milansys/E+/Getty Images; p. 22 Visuals Unlimited, Inc./Wally Eberhart/Visuals Unlimited/Getty Images.

Publisher's Cataloging Data

Dee, Willa.
Unearthing metamorphic rocks / Willa Dee. — 1st ed. — New York : Power Kids Press, c2014
        p. cm. — (Rocks: the hard facts)
Includes an index.
ISBN: 978-1-4777-2902-1 (Library Binding) — ISBN: 978-1-4777-2991-5 (Paperback) —
ISBN: 978-1-4777-3061-4 (6-pack)
1. Metamorphic rocks—Juvenile literature. 2. Rocks—Analysis–Juvenile literature. I. Title.
QE475.D44 2014
552.'4
Manufactured in the United States of America

CPSIA Compliance Information: Batch #W14PK4: For Further Information contact Rosen Publishing, New York, New York at 1-800-237-9932

CONTENTS

Changing Forms..4

Heat and Pressure 6

Inside Earth's Crust..8

Minerals and Crystals 10

Hot, Moving Water..12

Close to Magma 14

Grouping Metamorphic Rocks..16

Foliated Rocks..18

Nonfoliated Rocks 20

Part of the Cycle..22

Glossary 23

Index..24

Websites..24

CHANGING FORMS

Metamorphic rocks are one of Earth's three kinds of rocks. The other two kinds are igneous rocks and sedimentary rocks. Much of Earth's crust is made up of metamorphic rocks. The crust is Earth's top layer.

Many metamorphic rocks are very old. For example, the Acasta Gneiss in northwestern Canada is nearly four billion years old!

This picture shows rose quartzite, a type of metamorphic rock. Rose quartzite is named for its color, which can be pale pink to rose red.

However, all metamorphic rocks were once sedimentary, igneous, or different metamorphic rocks. If a rock is **exposed** to heat or pressure for a long time but does not melt, it will change into a metamorphic rock. This change can take millions of years!

You might not want to touch these metamorphic rocks. They are in Death Valley National Park, in California, which holds the record for the highest recorded temperature on Earth.

Metamorphic rock can form from igneous rocks, sedimentary rocks, or existing metamorphic rocks. Rocks change into metamorphic rock if they are put under stress. Over time, this stress makes the structure, or makeup, of the rock go through changes.

When a meteorite hits Earth, it can change sedimentary and igneous rock into metamorphic rock. It can also create a crater, like this one, which is in Death Valley, in California.

When Earth's plates move toward each other, rocks can break apart and create faults. When rocks on each side of the fault grind together, earthquakes can occur.

High heat is a force that puts rocks under stress. Another force is pressure. Pressure happens when something pushes down on or presses against something else.

One place rocks are exposed to high heat and pressure is deep within Earth's crust. Pressure is found where Earth's **plates** move toward each other as well. **Meteorites** also create pressure when they hit Earth's **surface**.

INSIDE EARTH'S CRUST

The process of rock changing into metamorphic rock is called metamorphism. There are different kinds of metamorphism. Most metamorphic rock is formed from heat and pressure within Earth's crust. This is called regional metamorphism.

Heat in Earth's crust is created by magma. Magma is **molten** rock found below Earth's crust. Pockets of magma are also trapped within the crust.

Erta Ale is the most active volcano in Ethiopia. When magma erupts from a volcano, it turns into lava.

Above: This diagram allows us to see what is underneath Earth's surface. The yellow area in the bottom is magma.
Right: Magma and lava are hot enough to make light and smoke come through cracks in Earth's crust!

The heat from this magma makes large areas of the crust very hot. Pressure comes from the layers of rock that make up Earth's crust. These layers push down on the layers below them. The heat and pressure change rock through the process of regional metamorphism.

MINERALS AND CRYSTALS

All rocks are made up of **minerals**. Some rocks are made up of just one kind of mineral. Others are made up of a combination of minerals. The minerals in a rock form crystals. In some rocks, you can easily see crystals with just your eyes. In other rocks, the crystals are too small to see without a **microscope**.

This picture shows schist, a type of metamorphic rock. Schist is used to build decorative walls and walkways in gardens.

The sedimentary rock in the Conch Bar Caves, in the Bahamas, is turning into marble through the process of metamorphism.

When a rock becomes a metamorphic rock, its crystals change. First, the stress from the heat and pressure break down the rock's minerals. Over time, mineral crystals regrow in different forms. This is called recrystallization. In the end, the rocks have totally different structures than they did before!

HOT, MOVING WATER

Metamorphic rock can also form when very hot water **circulates** through Earth's crust. There, the water moves through fractures, or cracks, in rock. The heat from the water causes changes to the rock. This is called hydrothermal metamorphism.

Minerals and chemicals give rocks their color. Rocks can be one solid color or a combination of many colors, like the rock shown here.

This picture shows pegmatite rock. Pegmatite rocks can contain rare minerals and gemstones, such as aquamarine, apatite, topaz, fluorite, and tourmaline.

The minerals that form rock are made up of **chemicals**. Heat from the water destroys the rocks' minerals and breaks them back down into chemicals. Chemicals carried by the water can also be added to the rock's existing chemicals. Then, these chemicals mix up to form different minerals. This means that the metamorphic rock that forms is made up of different minerals than the rock it came from!

CLOSE TO MAGMA

Another way metamorphic rock can form is through contact metamorphism. This kind of metamorphism happens when rock comes into contact with magma.

Below left: This marble was created when magma heated intrusive igneous rocks. This process is called contact metamorphism. Contact metamorphism is also called thermal metamorphism because it involves heat. *Below right*: This picture shows Mount Gould, in Montana. The darker layer toward the top is an igneous intrusion in sedimentary rock.

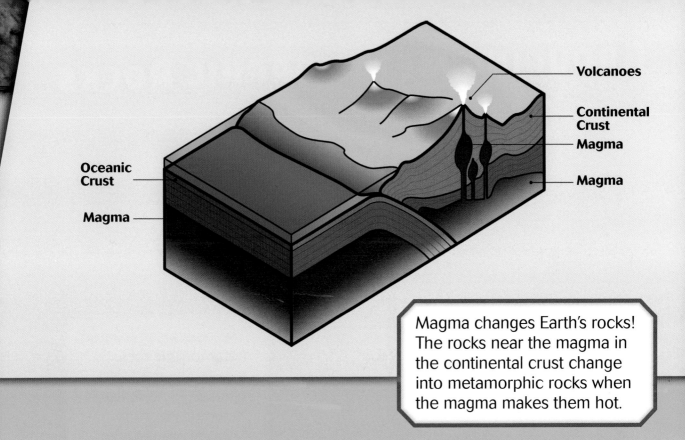

Oceanic Crust

Magma

Volcanoes

Continental Crust

Magma

Magma

Magma changes Earth's rocks! The rocks near the magma in the continental crust change into metamorphic rocks when the magma makes them hot.

The magma pushes up through cracks in an existing rock formation. However, the magma does not turn into metamorphic rock. Instead, it cools down and becomes a kind of igneous rock formation. This formation is called an igneous intrusion. Before the magma cools down, though, it gives off a lot of heat to the rock right around it. The force of this heat bakes that rock until it turns into metamorphic rock.

GROUPING METAMORPHIC ROCKS

When a rock changes into a metamorphic rock from a different kind of rock, many things about the rock change. The way the rock looks changes. It might have a different color or **texture**. The rock's crystal structures change. Sometimes, the minerals that make up the rock even change. Geologists classify metamorphic rocks, or put them into groups, by looking at these changes. Geologists are scientists who study rocks.

> The minerals in foliated metamorphic rock (top) are layered. The minerals in nonfoliated metamorphic rock (bottom) are random.

One way to classify a metamorphic rock is by texture. Metamorphic rocks can either have a foliated or nonfoliated texture. These textures have to do with how the minerals in the rock line up.

17

FOLIATED ROCKS

Foliated rocks are made up of flat or long crystal **grains** that form bands or layers. This happens when pressure squeezes the grains until they line up.

One kind of foliated metamorphic rock is gneiss. Gneiss is a coarse-grained rock. This means the minerals in the rock have formed crystals large enough to see. Gneiss has bands of pink and gray mineral crystals.

This picture shows gneiss, a type of foliated metamorphic rock. You can see crystals in gneiss because it is a coarse-grained rock.

Slate is a fine-grained foliated rock. It is made up of grains that are too small to see. Slate is often black or dark gray. It can be split into sheets.

Schist is a foliated rock with a scaly appearance. This comes from the mineral mica. Mica has platelike grains.

You cannot see crystals in this shale. It is the finest-grained foliated metamorphic rock.

NONFOLIATED ROCKS

Nonfoliated rocks are made up of mineral grains that are not flat or long. No matter how much pressure is put on these grains, they do not line up! This means that these rocks do not have bands or layers. However, they may have random lines or streaks.

The Taj Mahal, shown here, is a mausoleum, or tomb, in India. The Taj Mahal is made out of marble, which is a type of nonfoliated metamorphic rock.

Above: This is what marble looks like before it is smoothed down to make buildings like the Taj Mahal. *Right*: This rock turned from sandstone into quartzite.

Marble is a nonfoliated rock. Marble is formed when limestone, a sedimentary rock, is put under a lot of pressure. It is often white with flecks or streaks of red, green, gray, or black.

Quartzite is a white or gray nonfoliated rock. It is formed when sandstone is heated or put under pressure.

PART OF THE CYCLE

Metamorphic rocks are part of Earth's rock cycle. Sedimentary rocks and igneous rocks are, too! Through the rock cycle, old rocks are destroyed and **recycled** into new rocks.

If a metamorphic rock gets so hot it melts, it can become an igneous rock. If it reaches Earth's surface and is broken down into tiny pieces, those pieces can be pressed down into sedimentary rock. This cycle can take thousands or millions of years. Earth's rocks are always changing!

This picture shows several metamorphic rocks. Gneiss, slate, and schist are foliated metamorphic rocks. Marble and quartzite are nonfoliated rocks.

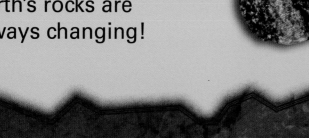

MARBLE

SLATE

QUARTZITE

GNEISS

SCHIST

GLOSSARY

chemicals (KEH-mih-kulz) Matter that can be mixed with other matter to cause changes.

circulates (SER-kyuh-layts) Moves about or flows freely.

exposed (ik-SPOHZD) Put into contact with.

grains (GRAYNZ) Small hard parts or crystals.

meteorites (MEE-tee-uh-ryts) Rocks from outer space that reach Earth's surface.

microscope (MY-kruh-skohp) An instrument used to see very small things.

minerals (MIN-rulz) Natural matter that is not animals, plants, or other living things.

molten (MOHL-ten) Made liquid by heat.

plates (PLAYTS) The moving pieces of Earth's crust, the top layer of Earth.

recycled (ree-SY-kuld) Used something again in a different way.

surface (SER-fes) The outside of anything.

texture (TEKS-chur) How something feels when you touch it.

INDEX

C
change(s), 5–6,
    12, 16
cracks, 12, 15
crust, 4, 7–9, 12

F
force, 7, 15
forms, 11

H
heat, 5, 7–9, 11–13,
    15

I
igneous intrusion,
    15

L
layer(s), 4, 9, 18, 20

M
magma, 8–9, 14–15
meteorites, 7
metamorphism, 8–9,
    12, 14
microscope, 10

P
plates, 7
pressure, 5, 7–9, 11,
    18, 20–21

S
scientists, 16
stress, 6–7, 11
structure(s), 6, 11, 16
surface, 7, 22

T
texture, 16

WEBSITES

Due to the changing nature of Internet links, PowerKids Press has developed an online list of websites related to the subject of this book. This site is updated regularly. Please use this link to access the list:
www.powerkidslinks.com/rthf/metam/